The Four Noble Truths

Venerable Ajahn Sumedho

For free distribution.

Publications from Amaravati are for free distribution. In most cases, this is made possible through offerings from individuals or groups, given specifically for the publication of Buddhist teachings. Further information is available from the address below.

Sabbadānaṁ dhammadānaṁ jināti
'The gift of Dhamma surpasses all other gifts.'

© Amaravati Publications 1992

Amaravati Publications
Amaravati Buddhist Centre
Great Gaddesden
Hemel Hempstead
Hertfordshire HP1 3BZ
England   ISBN 1 870205 10 3

Contents

A Handful of Leaves

The Blessed One was once living at Kosambi in a wood of simsapa trees. He picked up a few leaves in his hand, and he asked the bhikkhus, 'How do you conceive this, bhikkhus, which is more, the few leaves that I have picked up in my hand or those on the trees in the wood?

'The leaves that the Blessed One has picked up in his hand are few, Lord; those in the wood are far more.'

'So too, bhikkhus, the things that I have known by direct knowledge are more; the things that I have told you are only a few. Why have I not told them? Because they bring no benefit, no advancement in the Holy Life, and because they do not lead to dispassion, to fading, to ceasing, to stilling, to direct knowledge, to enlightenment, to Nibbana. That is why I have not told them. And what have I told you? This is suffering; this is the origin of suffering; this is the cessation of suffering; this is the way leading to the cessation of suffering. That is what I have told you. Why have I told it? Because it brings benefit, and advancement in the Holy Life, and because it leads to dispassion, to fading, to ceasing, to stilling, to direct knowledge, to enlightenment, to Nibbana. So bhikkhus, let your task be this: This is suffering, this is the origin of suffering, this is the cessation of suffering, this is the way leading to the cessation of suffering.' [Samyutta Nikaya, LVI, 31]

PREFACE

This small booklet was compiled and edited from talks given by Venerable Ajahn Sumedho on the central teaching of the Buddha: that the unhappiness of humanity can be overcome through spiritual means.

The teaching is conveyed through the Buddha's Four Noble Truths, first expounded in 528 B.C. in the Deer Park at Sarnath near Varanasi and kept alive in the Buddhist world ever since.

Venerable Ajahn Sumedho is a bhikkhu (mendicant monk) of the Theravada tradition of Buddhism. He was ordained in Thailand in 1966 and trained there for ten years. He is currently the Abbot of the Amaravati Buddhist Centre as well as teacher and spiritual guide to many bhikkhus, Buddhist nuns and lay people.

This booklet has been made available through the voluntary efforts of many people for the welfare of others.

Note on the Text:
The first exposition of the Four Noble Truths was a discourse (*sutta*) called Dhammacakkappavattana Sutta – literally, 'the discourse that sets the vehicle of the teaching in motion'. Extracts from this are quoted at the beginning of each chapter describing the Four Truths. The reference quoted is to the section in the books of the scriptures where this discourse can be found. However, the theme of the Four Noble Truths recurs many times, for example in the quotation that appears at the beginning of the Introduction.

INTRODUCTION

That both I and you have had to travel and trudge through
this long round is owing to our not discovering,
not penetrating four truths. What four?
They are: The Noble Truth of Suffering,
The Noble Truth of the Origin of Suffering, The Noble Truth
of the Cessation of Suffering, and The Noble Truth of the Way
Leading to the Cessation of Suffering.
[Digha Nikaya, Sutta 16]

The Dhammacakkappavattana Sutta, the Buddha's teaching on the Four Noble Truths, has been the main reference that I have used for my practice over the years. It is the teaching we used in our monastery in Thailand. The Theravada school of Buddhism regards this sutta as the quintessence of the teaching of the Buddha. This one sutta contains all that is necessary for understanding Dhamma and for enlightenment.

Though the Dhammacakkappavattana Sutta is considered to be the first sermon the Buddha gave after his enlightenment, I sometimes like to think that he gave his first sermon when he met an ascetic on the way to Varanasi. After his enlightenment in Bodh Gaya, the Buddha thought: 'This is such a subtle teaching. I cannot possibly convey in words what I have discovered so I will not teach. I will just sit under the Bodhi tree for the rest of my life.'

For me this is a very tempting idea, just to go off and live alone and not have to deal with the problems of society. However, while the Buddha was thinking this way, Brahma Sahampati, the creator deity in Hinduism, came to the Buddha and convinced him that he should go and teach. Brahma Sahampati persuaded the Buddha that there were beings who would understand, beings who had only a little dust in their eyes. So the Buddha's teaching was aimed toward those with only a little dust in their eyes – I'm sure he did not think it would become a mass, popular movement.

After Brahma Sahampati's visit, the Buddha was on his way from Bodh Gaya to Varanasi when he met an ascetic who was impressed by his radiant appearance. The ascetic said, 'What is it that you have discovered?' and the Buddha responded: 'I am the perfectly enlightened one, the Arahant, the Buddha.'

I like to consider this his first sermon. It was a failure because the man listening thought the Buddha had been practising too hard and was overestimating himself. If somebody said those words to us, I'm sure we would react similarly. What would you do if I said, 'I am the perfectly enlightened one'?

Actually, the Buddha's statement was a very accurate, precise teaching. It is the perfect teaching, but people cannot understand it. They tend to misunderstand and to think it comes from an ego because people are always interpreting everything from their egos. 'I am the perfectly enlightened one' may sound like an egotistical statement, but isn't it really purely transcendent? That statement: 'I am the Buddha, the perfectly enlightened one', is interesting to contemplate because it connects the use of 'I am' with superlative attainments or realisations. In any case, the result of the Buddha's first teaching was that the listener could not understand it and walked away.

✧ ✧ ✧

9

Later, the Buddha met his five former companions in the Deer Park in Varanasi. All five were very sincerely dedicated to strict asceticism. They had been disillusioned with the Buddha earlier because they thought he had become insincere in his practice. This was because the Buddha, before he was enlightened, had begun to realise that strict asceticism was in no way conducive towards an enlightened state so he was no longer practising in that way. These five friends thought he was taking it easy: maybe they saw him eating milk rice, which would perhaps be comparable to eating ice cream these days. If you are an ascetic and you see a monk eating ice cream, you might lose your faith in him because you think that monks should be eating nettle soup. If you really loved asceticism and you saw me eating a dish of ice cream, you would have no faith in Ajahn Sumedho any more. That is the way the human mind works; we tend to admire impressive feats of self-torture and denial. When they lost faith in him, these five friends or disciples left the Buddha – which gave him the chance to sit under the Bodhi tree and be enlightened.

Then, when they met the Buddha again in the Deer Park in Varanasi, the five thought at first, 'We know what *he's* like. Let's just not bother about him.' But as he came near, they all felt that there was something special about him. They stood up to make a place for him to sit down and he delivered his sermon on the Four Noble Truths.

This time, instead of saying 'I am the enlightened one', he said: 'There is suffering. There is the origin of suffering. There is the cessation of suffering. There is the path out of suffering.' Presented in this way, his teaching requires no acceptance or denial. If he had said 'I am the all-enlightened one', we would be forced to either agree or disagree – or just be bewildered. We wouldn't quite know how to look at that statement. However, by saying: 'There is suffering, there is a cause, there is an end of suffering, and there is the way out of suffering', he offered something for reflection: 'What do you mean by this?

What do you mean by suffering, its origin, cessation and the path?'

So we start contemplating it, thinking about it. With the statement: 'I am the all enlightened one', we might just argue about it. 'Is he really enlightened?' . . . 'I don't think so.' We would just argue; we are not ready for a teaching that is so direct. Obviously, the Buddha's first sermon was to somebody who still had a lot of dust in his eyes and it failed. So on the second occasion, he gave the teaching of the Four Noble Truths .

Now the Four Noble Truths are: there is suffering; there is a cause or origin of suffering; there is an end of suffering; and there is a path out of suffering which is the Eightfold Path. Each of these Truths has three aspects so all together there are twelve insights. In the Theravada school, an arahant, a perfected one, is one who has seen clearly the Four Noble Truths with their three aspects and twelve insights. 'Arahant' means a human being who understands the truth; it is applied mainly to the teaching of the Four Noble Truths.

For the First Noble Truth, 'There is suffering' is the first insight. What is that insight? We don't need to make it into anything grand; it is just the recognition: 'There is suffering.' That is a basic insight. The ignorant person says, 'I'm suffering. I don't want to suffer. I meditate and I go on retreats to get out of suffering, but I'm still suffering and I don't want to suffer. . . . How can I get out of suffering? What can I do to get rid of it?' But that is not the First Noble Truth; it is not: '*I* am suffering and *I* want to end it.' The insight is, 'There is suffering.'

Now you are looking at the pain or the anguish you feel – not from the perspective of 'It's mine' but as a reflection: 'There is this suffering, this *dukkha*.' It is coming from the reflective position of 'Buddha seeing the Dhamma.' The insight is simply the acknowledgement that there is this suffering without making it personal. That acknowledgement is an

11

important insight; just looking at mental anguish or physical pain and seeing it as *dukkha* rather than as personal misery – just seeing it as *dukkha* and not reacting to it in a habitual way.

The second insight of the First Noble Truth is: 'Suffering should be understood.' The second insight or aspect of each of the Noble Truths has the word 'should' in it: 'It should be understood.' The second insight, then, is that *dukkha* is something to understand. One should understand *dukkha*, not just try to get rid of it.

We can look at the word 'understanding' as 'standing under'. It is a common enough word but, in Pali, 'understanding' means to really accept the suffering, stand under or embrace it rather than just react to it. With any form of suffering – physical or mental – we usually just react, but with understanding we can really look at suffering; really accept it, really hold it and embrace it. So that is the second aspect, 'We should understand suffering.'

The third aspect of the First Noble Truth is: 'Suffering has been understood.' When you have actually practised with suffering – looking at it, accepting it, knowing it and letting it be the way it is – then there is the third aspect, 'Suffering has been understood', or, '*Dukkha* has been understood.' So these are the three aspects of the First Noble Truth: 'There is *dukkha*'; 'It is to be understood'; and, 'It has been understood.'

This is the pattern for the three aspects of each Noble Truth. There is the statement, then the prescription and then the result of having practised. One can also see it in terms of the Pali words *pariyatti*, *patipatti* and *pativedha*. *Pariyatti* is the theory or the statement, 'There is suffering.' *Patipatti* is the practice – actually practising with it; and *pativedha* is the result of the practice. This is what we call a reflective pattern; you are actually developing your mind in a very reflective way. A Buddha mind is a reflective mind that knows things as they are.

12

We use these Four Noble Truths for our development. We apply them to ordinary things in our lives, to ordinary attachments and obsessions of the mind. With these truths, we can investigate our attachments in order to have the insights. Through the Third Noble Truth, we can realise cessation, the end of suffering, and practise the Eightfold Path until there is understanding. When the Eightfold Path has been fully developed, one is an arahant, one has made it. Even though this sounds complicated – four truths, three aspects, twelve insights – it is quite simple. It is a tool for us to use to help us understand suffering and non-suffering.

Within the Buddhist world, there are not many Buddhists who use the Four Noble Truths any more, even in Thailand. People say, 'Oh yes, the Four Noble Truths – beginner's stuff.' Then they might use all kinds of *vipassana* techniques and become really obsessed with the sixteen stages before they get to the Noble Truths. I find it quite boggling that in the Buddhist world the really profound teaching has been dismissed as primitive Buddhism: 'That's for the little kids, the beginners. The advanced course is. . . .' They go into complicated theories and ideas – forgetting the most profound teaching.

The Four Noble Truths are a lifetime's reflection. It is not just a matter of realising the Four Noble Truths, the three aspects, and twelve stages and becoming an arahant on one retreat – and *then* going onto something advanced. The Four Noble Truths are not easy like that. They require an ongoing attitude of vigilance and they provide the context for a lifetime of examination.

---

*i.e. meditation exercises – see pages 62-64

THE FIRST NOBLE TRUTH

What is the Noble Truth of Suffering? Birth is suffering, ageing
is suffering, sickness is suffering, dissociation from the loved is
suffering, not to get what one wants is suffering: in short the
five categories affected by clinging are suffering.
There is this Noble Truth of Suffering: such was the vision,
insight, wisdom, knowing and light that arose in me about things
not heard before.
This Noble Truth must be penetrated by fully understanding
suffering: such was the vision, insight, wisdom, knowing, and
light that arose in me about things not heard before.
This Noble Truth has been penetrated by fully understanding
suffering: such was the vision, insight, wisdom, knowing and
light that arose in me about things not heard before.
[Samyutta Nikaya LVI, 11]

The First Noble Truth with its three aspects is: 'There
is suffering, *dukkha*. *Dukkha* should be understood.
Dukkha has been understood.'

This is a very skilful teaching because it is expressed in a
simple formula which is easy to remember, and it also applies
to everything that you can possibly experience or do or think
concerning the past, the present or the future.

Suffering or *dukkha* is the common bond we all share.
Everybody everywhere suffers. Human beings suffered in the
past, in ancient India; they suffer in modern Britain; and in

the future, human beings will also suffer. . . . What do we have in common with Queen Elizabeth? – we suffer. With a tramp in Charing Cross, what do we have in common? – suffering. It includes all levels from the most privileged human beings to the most desperate and underprivileged ones, and all ranges in between. Everybody everywhere suffers. It is a bond we have with each other, something we all understand.

When we talk about our human suffering, it brings out our compassionate tendencies. But when we talk about our opinions, about what I think and what you think about politics and religion, then we can get into wars. I remember seeing a film in London about ten years ago. It tried to portray Russian people as human beings by showing Russian women with babies and Russian men taking their children out for picnics. At the time, this presentation of the Russian people was unusual because most of the propaganda of the West made them out to be titanic monsters or cold-hearted, reptilian people – and so you never thought of them as human beings. If you want to kill people, you have to make them out to be that way; you cannot very well kill somebody if you realise they suffer the way you do. You have to think that they are cold-hearted, immoral, worthless and bad, and that it is better to get rid of them. You have to think that they are evil and that it is good to get rid of evil. With this attitude, you might feel justified in bombing and machine-gunning them. If you keep in mind our common bond of suffering, that makes you quite incapable of doing those things.

The First Noble Truth is not a dismal metaphysical statement saying that everything is suffering. Notice that there is a difference between a metaphysical doctrine in which you are making a statement about The Absolute and a Noble Truth which is a reflection. A Noble Truth is a truth to reflect upon; it is not an absolute; it is not The Absolute. This is where Western people get very confused because they interpret this Noble Truth as a kind of metaphysical truth of Buddhism – but it was never meant to be that.

15

You can see that the First Noble Truth is not an absolute statement because of the Fourth Noble Truth, which is the way of non-suffering. You cannot have absolute suffering and then have a way out of it, can you? That doesn't make sense. Yet some people will pick up on the First Noble Truth and say that the Buddha taught that everything is suffering.

The Pali word, *dukkha*, means 'incapable of satisfying' or 'not able to bear or withstand anything': always changing, incapable of truly fulfilling us or making us happy. The sensual world is like that, a vibration in nature. It would, in fact, be terrible if we did find satisfaction in the sensory world because then we wouldn't search beyond it; we'd just be bound to it. However, as we awaken to this *dukkha*, we begin to find the way out so that we are no longer constantly trapped in sensory consciousness.

SUFFERING AND SELF-VIEW

It is important to reflect upon the phrasing of the First Noble Truth. It is phrased in a very clear way: 'There is suffering,' rather than, 'I suffer.' Psychologically, that reflection is a much more skilful way to put it. We tend to interpret our suffering as 'I'm really suffering. I suffer a lot – and I don't want to suffer.' This is the way our thinking mind is conditioned.

'I am suffering' always conveys the sense of 'I am somebody who is suffering a lot. This suffering is mine; I've had a lot of suffering in my life.' Then the whole process, the association with one's self and one's memory, takes off. You remember what happened when you were a baby. . . and so on.

But note, we are not saying there is someone who has suffering. It is not personal suffering anymore when we see it as 'There is suffering'. It is not: 'Oh poor me, why do I have to suffer so much? What did I do to deserve this? Why do I have to get old? Why do I have to have sorrow, pain, grief and despair? It is not fair! I do not want it. I only want happiness and security.' This kind of thinking comes from ignorance

16

which complicates everything and results in personality problems.

To let go of suffering, we have to admit it into consciousness. But the admission in Buddhist meditation is not from a position of: '*I am* suffering' but rather, '*There is* the presence of suffering' because we are not trying to identify with the problem but simply acknowledge that there is one. It is unskilful to think in terms of: 'I am an angry person; I get angry so easily; how do I get rid of it?' – that triggers off all the underlying assumptions of a self and it is very hard to get any perspective on that. It becomes very confused because the sense of *my* problems or *my* thoughts takes us very easily to suppression or to making judgements about it and criticising ourselves. We tend to grasp and identify rather than to observe, witness and understand things as they are. When you are just admitting that there is this feeling of confusion, that there is this greed or anger, then there is an honest reflection on the way it is and you have taken out all the underlying assumptions – or at least undermined them.

So do not grasp these things as personal faults but keep contemplating these conditions as impermanent, unsatisfactory and non-self. Keep reflecting, seeing them as they are. The tendency is to view life from the sense that these are *my* problems, and that one is being very honest and forthright in admitting this. Then our life tends to reaffirm that because we keep operating from that wrong assumption. But that very viewpoint is impermanent, unsatisfactory and non-self.

'There is suffering' is a very clear, precise acknowledgement that at this time, there is some feeling of unhappiness. It can range from anguish and despair to mild irritation; *dukkha* does not necessarily mean severe suffering. You do not have to be brutalised by life; you do not have to come from Auschwitz or Belsen to say that there is suffering. Even Queen Elizabeth could say, 'There is suffering.' I'm sure she has moments of great anguish and despair or, at least, moments of irritation.

17

The sensory world is a sensitive experience. It means you are always being exposed to pleasure and pain and the dualism of *samsara*. It is like being in something that is very vulnerable and picking up everything that happens to come in contact with these bodies and their senses. That is the way it is. That is the result of birth.

DENIAL OF SUFFERING

Suffering is something we usually do not want to know – we just want to get rid of it. As soon as there is any inconvenience or annoyance, the tendency of an unawakened human being is to get rid of it or suppress it. One can see why modern society is so caught up in seeking pleasures and delights in what is new, exciting or romantic. We tend to emphasise the beauties and pleasures of youth whilst the ugly side of life – old age, sickness, death, boredom, despair and depression, are pushed aside. When we find ourselves with something we do not like, we try to get away from it to something we do like. If we feel boredom, we go to something interesting. If we feel frightened, we try to find safety. This is a perfectly natural thing to do. We are associated with that pleasure/pain principle of being attracted and repelled. So if the mind is not full and receptive, then it is selective – it selects what it likes and tries to suppress what it does not like. Much of our experience has to be suppressed because a lot of what we are inevitably involved with is unpleasant in some way.

If anything unpleasant arises, we say, 'Run away!' If anyone gets in our way, we say, 'Kill him!' This tendency is often apparent in what our governments do. . . . Frightening, isn't it, when you think of the kind of people who run our countries – because they are still very ignorant and unenlightened. But that is the way it is. The ignorant mind thinks of extermination: 'Here's a mosquito; kill it!', 'These ants are taking over the room; spray them with ant killer!' There is a company in Britain called Rent-o-Kil. I don't know if it is a kind of British

18

mafia or what, but it specialises in killing pests – however you want to interpret the word 'pests'.

MORALITY AND COMPASSION

That is why we have to have laws such as, 'I will refrain from intentionally killing,' because our instinctual nature is to kill: if it is in the way, kill it. You can see this in the animal kingdom. We are quite predatory creatures ourselves; we think we are civilised but we have a really bloody history – literally. It is just filled with endless slaughters and justification for all kinds of iniquities against other human beings – not to mention animals – and it is all because of this basic ignorance, this unreflecting human mind that tells us to annihilate what is in our way.

However, with reflection we are changing that; we are transcending that basic instinctual, animal pattern. We are not just being law-abiding puppets of society, afraid to kill because we are afraid of being punished. Now we are really taking on responsibility. We respect the lives of other creatures, even the lives of insects and creatures we do not like. Nobody is ever going to like mosquitoes or ants, but we can reflect on the fact that they have a right to live. That is a reflection of the mind; it is not just a reaction: 'Where is the insecticide spray.' *I* also don't like to see ants crawling over *my* floor; my first reaction is, 'Where's the insecticide spray.' But then the reflective mind shows me that even though these creatures are annoying me and I would rather they go away, they have a right to exist. That is a reflection of the human mind.

The same applies to unpleasant mind states. So when you are experiencing anger, rather than saying: 'Oh, here I go – angry again!' we reflect: 'There is anger'. Just like with fear – if you start seeing it as my mother's fear or my father's fear or the dog's fear or my fear, then it all becomes a sticky web of different creatures related in some ways, unrelated in others; and it becomes difficult to have any real understanding. And yet, the fear in this being and the fear in that mangy cur is the

19

same thing. 'There is fear'. It is just that. The fear that I have experienced is no different from the fear others have. So this is where we have compassion even for mangy old dogs. We understand that fear is as horrible for mangy dogs as it is for us. When a dog is kicked with a heavy boot and you are kicked with a heavy boot, that feeling of pain is the same. Pain is just pain, cold is just cold, anger is just anger. It is not mine but rather: 'There is pain.' This is a skilful use of thinking that helps us to see things more clearly rather than reinforcing the personal view. Then as a result of recognising the state of suffering – that there is suffering – the second insight of this First Noble Truth comes: 'It should be understood'. This suffering is to be investigated.

TO INVESTIGATE SUFFERING

I encourage you to try to understand *dukkha*: to really look at, stand under and accept your suffering. Try to understand it when you are feeling physical pain or despair and anguish or hatred and aversion – whatever form it takes, whatever quality it has, whether it is extreme or slight. This teaching does not mean that to get enlightened you have to be utterly and totally miserable. You do not have to have everything taken away from you or be tortured on the rack; it means being able to look at suffering, even if it is just a mild feeling of discontent, and understand it.

It is easy to find a scapegoat for our problems. 'If my mother had really loved me or if everyone around me had been truly wise, and fully dedicated towards providing a perfect environment for me, then I would not have the emotional problems I have now.' This is really silly! Yet that is how some people actually look at the world, thinking that they are confused and miserable because they did not get a fair deal. But with this formula of the First Noble Truth, even if we have had a pretty miserable life, what we are looking at is not that suffering which comes from out there, but what we create in our own minds around it. This is an awakening in a person – an awakening to the Truth of suffering. And it is a Noble Truth because it is no longer blaming the suffering that we are experiencing on others. Thus, the Buddhist approach is quite unique whith respect to other religions because the emphasis is on the way out of suffering through wisdom, freedom from all delusion, rather than the attainment of some blissful state or union with the Ultimate.

Now I am not saying that others are never the source of our frustration and irritation, but what we are pointing at with this teaching is our own reaction to life. If somebody is being nasty to you or deliberately and malevolently trying to cause you to suffer, and you think it is that person who is making you suffer, you still have not understood this First Noble Truth. Even if he is pulling out your fingernails or doing other terrible things to you – as long as you think that you are suffering because of that person, you have not understood this First Noble Truth. To understand suffering is to see clearly that it is our reaction to the person pulling out our fingernails, 'I hate you,' that is suffering. The actual pulling out of one's fingernails is painful, but the suffering involves 'I hate you,' and 'How can you do this to me,' and 'I'll never forgive you.'

However, don't wait for somebody to pull out your finger-nails in order to practise with the First Noble Truth. Try it with little things, like somebody being insensitive or rude or ignor-ing you. If you are suffering because that person has slighted you or offended you in some way, you can work with that. There are many times in daily life when we can be offended or upset. We can feel annoyed or irritated just by the way somebody walks or looks, at least I can. Sometimes you can notice yourself feeling aversion just because of the way somebody walks or because they don't do something that they should – one can get very upset and angry about things like that. The person has not really harmed you or done anything to you, like pulling out your fingernails, but you still suffer. If you cannot look at suffering in these simple cases, you will

21

never be able to be so heroic as to do it if ever somebody does actually pull out your fingernails!

We work with the little dissatisfactions in the ordinariness of life. We look at the way we can be hurt and offended or annoyed and irritated by the neighbours, by the people we live with, by Mrs. Thatcher, by the way things are or by ourselves. We know that this suffering should be understood. We practise by really looking at suffering as an object and understanding: 'This is suffering.' So we have the insightful understanding of suffering.

PLEASURE AND DISPLEASURE

We can investigate: Where has this hedonistic seeking of pleasure as an end in itself brought us? It has continued now for several decades but is humanity any happier as a result? It seems that nowadays we have been given the right and freedom to do anything we like with drugs, sex, travel and so on – anything goes; anything is allowed; nothing is forbidden. You have to do something *really* obscene, *really* violent, before you'll be ostracised. But has being able to follow our impulses made us any happier or more relaxed and contented? In fact, it has tended to make us very selfish; we don't think about how our actions might affect others. We tend to think only about ourselves: me and *my* happiness, *my* freedom and *my* rights. So I become a terrible nuisance, a source of great frustration, annoyance and misery for the people around me. If I think I can do anything I want or say anything I feel like saying, even at the expense of others, then I'm a person who is nothing but a nuisance to society.

When the sense of 'what *I* want' and 'what *I* think should and should not be' arises, and we wish to delight in all the pleasures of life, we inevitably get upset because life seems so hopeless and everything seems to go wrong. We just get whirled about by life – just running around in states of fear and desire. And even when we get everything we want, we will think there is something missing, something incomplete yet.

22

So even when life is at its best, there is still this sense of suffering – something yet to be done, some kind of doubt or fear haunting us.

For example, I've always liked beautiful scenery. Once during a retreat that I led in Switzerland, I was taken to some beautiful mountains and noticed that there was always a sense of anguish in my mind because there was so much beauty, a continual flow of beautiful sights. I had the feeling of wanting to hold on to everything, that I had to keep alert all the time in order to consume everything with my eyes. It was really wearing me out! Now that was *dukkha*, wasn't it?

I find that if I do things heedlessly – even something quite harmless like looking at beautiful mountains – if I'm just reaching out and trying to hold on to something, it always brings an unpleasant feeling. How *can* you hold on to the Jungfrau and the Eiger? The best you can do is to take a picture of it, trying to capture everything on a piece of paper. That's *dukkha*; if you want to hold on to something which is beautiful because you don't want to be separated from it – *that* is suffering.

Having to be in situations you don't like is also suffering. For example, I never liked riding in the Underground in London. I'd complain about it: 'I don't want to go on the underground with those awful posters and dingy Underground stations. I don't want to be packed into those little trains under the ground.' I found it a totally unpleasant experience. But I'd listen to this complaining, moaning voice – the suffering of not wanting to be with something unpleasant. Then, having contemplated this, I stopped making anything of it so that I could be with the unpleasant and un-beautiful without suffering about it. I realised that it's just that way and it's *all right*. We needn't make problems – either about being in a dingy Underground station or about looking at beautiful scenery. Things are as they are, so we can recognise and appreciate them in their changing forms without grasping. Grasping is wanting to hold on to something we like; wanting to get rid of something we don't like; or wanting to get something we don't have.

We can also suffer a lot because of other people. I remember that in Thailand I used to have quite negative thoughts about one of the monks. Then he'd do something and I'd think, 'He shouldn't do that,' or he'd say something, 'He shouldn't say that!' I'd carry this monk around in my mind and then, even if I went to some other place, I'd think of that monk; the perception of him would arise and the same reactions would come: 'Do you remember when he said this and when he did that?' and: 'He shouldn't have said that and he shouldn't have done that.'

Having found a teacher like Ajahn Chah, I remember wanting him to be perfect. I'd think, 'Oh, he's a marvellous teacher – marvellous!' But then he might do something that would upset me and I'd think, 'I don't want him to do anything that upsets me because I like to think of him as being marvellous.' That was like saying, 'Ajahn Chah, be marvellous for me *all* the time. Don't *ever* do anything that will put any kind of negative thought into my mind.' So even when you find somebody that you really respect and love, there's still the suffering of attachment. Inevitably, they will do or say some--thing that you're not going to like or approve of, causing you some kind of doubt – and you'll suffer.

At one time, several American monks came to Wat Pah Pong, our monastery in Northeastern Thailand. They were very critical and it seemed that they only saw what was wrong with it. They didn't think Ajahn Chah was a very good teacher and they didn't like the monastery. I felt a great anger and hatred arising because they were criticising something that I loved. I felt indignant – 'Well, if you don't like it, get out of here. He's the finest teacher in the world and if you can't see that then just GO!' That kind of attachment – being in love or being devoted – is suffering because if something or someone you love or like is criticised, you feel angry and indignant.

INSIGHT IN SITUATIONS

Sometimes insight arises at the most unexpected times. This happened to me while living at Wat Pah Pong. The Northeastern part of Thailand is not the most beautiful or desirable place in the world with its scrubby forests and flat plain; it also gets extremely hot during the hot season. We'd have to go out in the heat of the mid-afternoon before each of the Observance Days* and sweep the leaves off the paths. There were vast areas to sweep. We would spend the whole afternoon in the hot sun, sweating and sweeping the leaves into piles with crude brooms; this was one of our duties. I didn't like doing this. I'd think, 'I don't want to do this. I didn't come here to sweep the leaves off the ground; I came here to get enlightened – and instead they have me sweeping leaves off the ground. Besides, it's hot and I have a fair skin; I might get skin cancer from being out here in a hot climate.'

I was standing out there one afternoon, feeling really miserable, thinking, 'What am I doing here? Why did I come here? Why am I staying here?' There I stood with my long crude broom and absolutely no energy, feeling sorry for myself and hating everything. Then Ajahn Chah came up, smiled at me and said, 'Wat Pah Pong is a lot of suffering, isn't it?' and walked away. So I thought, 'Why did he say that?' and, 'Actually, you know, it's not all that bad.' He got me to contemplate: Is sweeping the leaves really that unpleasant? . . . No, it's not. It's a kind of neutral thing; you sweep the leaves, and it's neither here nor there. . . . Is sweating all that terrible? Is it really a miserable, humiliating experience? Is it really as bad as I'm pretending it is? . . . No – sweating is all right, it's a perfectly natural thing to be doing. And I don't have skin cancer and the people at Wat Pah Pong are very nice. The teacher is a very kind wise man. The monks have treated me well. The lay people come and give me food to eat, and. . . . What am I complaining about?'

---

* For explanations of terms marked thus * see glossary at end.

Reflecting upon the actual experience of being there, I thought, 'I'm all right. People respect me, I'm treated well. I'm being taught by pleasant people in a very pleasant country. There's nothing really wrong with anything, except *me*; I'm making a problem out of it because I don't want to sweat and I don't want to sweep leaves.' Then I had a very clear insight. I suddenly perceived something in me which was always complaining and criticising, and which was preventing me from ever giving myself to anything or offering myself to any situation.

Another experience I learned from was the custom of washing the feet of the senior monks when they returned from the almsround. After they walked barefoot through the villages and rice paddies, their feet would be muddy. There were foot baths outside the dining hall. When Ajahn Chah would come, all the monks – maybe twenty or thirty of them – would rush out and wash Ajahn Chah's feet. When I first saw this I thought, 'I'm not going to do that – not me!' Then the next day, thirty monks rushed out as soon as Ajahn Chah appeared and washed his feet – I thought, 'What a *stupid* thing to be doing – thirty monks washing one man's feet. I'm not going to do *that*.' The day after that, the reaction became even more violent . . . thirty monks rushed out and washed Ajahn Chah's feet and. . . . 'That really *angers* me, I'm fed up with it! I just feel that is the most stupid thing I've *ever* seen – thirty men going out to wash one man's feet! He probably thinks he deserves it, you know – it's really building up his ego. He's probably got an enormous ego, having so many people wash his feet every day. I'll *never* do that!'

I was beginning to build up a strong reaction, an overreaction. I would sit there really feeling miserable and angry. I'd look at the monks and I'd think, 'They all look stupid to me. I don't know what I'm doing here.'

But then I started listening and I thought, 'This is really an unpleasant frame of mind to be in. Is it anything to get upset about? They haven't made *me* do it. It's all right; there's

26

nothing wrong with thirty men washing one man's feet. It's not immoral or *bad* behaviour and maybe they enjoy it; maybe they want to do it – maybe it's all right to do that. . . . Maybe I should do it!' So the next morning, thirty-*one* monks ran out and washed Ajahn Chah's feet. There was no problem after that. It felt really good: that nasty thing in me had stopped.

We can reflect upon these things that arouse indignation and anger in us: is something really wrong with them or is it something *we* create *dukkha* about? Then we begin to understand the problems we create in our own lives and in the lives of the people around us.

With mindfulness, we are willing to bear with the whole of life; with the excitement and the boredom, the hope and the despair, the pleasure and the pain, the fascination and the weariness, the beginning and the ending, the birth and the death. We are willing to accept the whole of it in the mind rather than absorb into just the pleasant and suppress the unpleasant. The process of insight is the going to *dukkha*, looking at *dukkha*, admitting *dukkha*, recognising *dukkha* in all its forms. Then you are no longer just reacting in the habitual way of indulgence or suppression. And because of that, you can bear with suffering more, you can be more patient with it.

These teachings are not outside our experience. They are, in fact, reflections of our actual experience – not complicated intellectual issues. So really put effort into development rather than just getting stuck in a rut. How many times do you have to feel guilty about your abortion or the mistakes you have made in the past? Do you have to spend all your time just regurgitating the things that have happened to you in your life and indulging in endless speculation and analysis? Some people make themselves into such complicated personalities. If you just indulge in your memories and views and opinions, then you will always stay stuck in the world and never transcend it in any way.

You can let go of this burden if you are willing to use the teachings skilfully. Tell yourself: 'I'm not going to get caught in this any more; I refuse to participate in this game. I'm not going to give in to this mood.' Start putting yourself in the position of knowing: 'I know this is *dukkha*; there is *dukkha*.' It's really important to make this resolution to go where the suffering is and then abide with it. It is only by examining and confronting suffering in this way that one can hope to have the tremendous insight: 'This suffering has been understood.'

So these are the three aspects of the First Noble Truth. This is the formula that we must use and apply in reflection on our lives. Whenever you feel suffering, first make the recognition: 'There is suffering', then: 'It should be understood', and finally: 'It has been understood'. This understanding of *dukkha* is the insight into the First Noble Truth.

THE SECOND NOBLE TRUTH

*What is the Noble Truth of the Origin of Suffering? It is
craving which renews being and is accompanied by relish and
lust, relishing this and that: in other words, craving for sensual
desires, craving for being, craving for non-being. But whereon
does this craving arise and flourish? Wherever there is what
seems lovable and gratifying, thereon it arises and flourishes.
There is this Noble Truth of the Origin of Suffering: such was the
vision, insight, wisdom, knowing and light that
arose in me about things not heard before.
This Noble Truth must be penetrated to by abandoning
the origin of suffering. . . .
This Noble Truth has been penetrated to by abandoning the
origin of suffering: such was the vision, insight, wisdom, knowing
and light that arose in me about things not heard before.*
[Samyutta Nikaya LVI, 11]

The Second Noble Truth with its three aspects is:
'There is the origin of suffering, which is the attachment to desire. Desire should be let go of. Desire has been let
go of.'

The Second Noble Truth states that there is an origin of
suffering and that the origin of suffering is attachment to the
three kinds of desire: desire for sense pleasure (*kama tanha*),
desire to become (*bhava tanha*) and desire to get rid of (*vibhava*

29

tanha). This is the statement of the Second Noble Truth, the thesis, the *pariyatti*. This is what you contemplate: the origin of suffering is attachment to desire.

THREE KINDS OF DESIRE

Desire or *tanha* in Pali is an important thing to understand. What is desire? *Kama tanha* is very easy to understand. This kind of desire is wanting sense pleasures through the body or the other senses and always seeking things to excite or please your senses – that is *kama tanha*. You can really contemplate: what is it like when you have desire for pleasure? For example, when you are eating, if you are hungry and the food tastes delicious, you can be aware of wanting to take another bite. Notice that feeling when you are tasting something pleasant; and notice how you want more of it. Don't just believe this; try it out. Don't think you know it because it has been that way in the past. Try it out when you eat. Taste something delicious and see what happens: a desire arises for more. That is *kama tanha*.

We also contemplate the feeling of wanting to become something. But if there is ignorance, then when we are not seeking something delicious to eat or some beautiful music to listen to, we can be caught in a realm of ambition and attainment – the desire to *become*. We get caught in that movement of striving to become happy, seeking to become wealthy; or we might attempt to make our life feel important by endeavouring to make the world right. So note this sense of wanting to become something other than what you are right now.

Listen to the *bhava tanha* of your life: 'I want to practise meditation so I can become free from my pain. I want to become enlightened. I want to become a monk or a nun. I want to become enlightened as a lay person. I want to have a wife and children and a profession. I want to enjoy the sense world without having to give up anything and become an enlightened arahant too.'

30

When we get disillusioned with trying to become something, then there is the desire to *get rid of* things. So we contemplate *vibhava tanha*, the desire to get rid of: 'I want to get rid of my suffering. I want to get rid of my anger. I've got this anger and I want to get rid of it. I want to get rid of jealousy, fear and anxiety.' Notice this as a reflection on *vibhava tanha*. We are actually contemplating that within ourselves which wants to get rid of things; we are *not* trying to get rid of *vibhava tanha*. We are not taking a stand against the desire to get rid of things nor are we encouraging that desire. Instead, we are reflecting, 'It's like this; it feels like this to want to get rid of something; I've got to conquer my anger; I have to kill the Devil and get rid of my greed – then I will become. . . .' We can see from this train of thought that becoming and getting rid of are very much associated.

Bear in mind though that these three categories of *kama tanha*, *bhava tanha* and *vibhava tanha* are merely convenient ways of contemplating desire. They are not totally separate forms of desire but different aspects of it.

The second insight into the Second Noble Truth is: 'Desire should be let go of.' This is how letting go comes into our practice. You have an insight that desire should be let go of, but that insight is not a *desire* to let go of anything. If you are not very wise and are not really reflecting in your mind, you tend to follow the 'I want to get rid of, I want to let go of all my desires' – but this is just another desire. However, you can reflect upon it; you can see the desire to get rid of, the desire to become or the desire for sense pleasure. By understanding these three kinds of desire, you can let them go.

The Second Noble Truth does not ask you to think, 'I have a lot of sensual desires', or, 'I'm really ambitious. I'm really *bhava tanha* plus, plus, plus!' or, 'I'm a real nihilist. I just want out. I'm a real *vibhava tanha* fanatic. That's me.' The Second Noble Truth is not that. It is not about identifying with desires in any way; it's about *recognising* desire.

31

I used to spend a lot of time watching how much of my practice was desire to become something. For example, how much of the good intentions of my meditation practice as a monk was to become liked – how much of my relations with other monks or nuns or with lay people had to do with wanting to be liked and approved of. That is *bhava tanha* – desire for praise and success. As a monk, you have this *bhava tanha*: wanting people to understand everything and to appreciate the Dhamma. Even these subtle, almost noble, desires are *bhava tanha*.

Then there is *vibhava tanha* in spiritual life, which can be very self-righteous: 'I want to get rid of, annihilate and exterminate these defilements.' I really listened to myself thinking, 'I want to get rid of desire. I want to get rid of anger. I don't want to be frightened or jealous any more. I want to be brave. I want to have joy and gladness in my heart.'

This practice of Dhamma is not one of hating oneself for having such thoughts, but really seeing that these are conditioned into the mind. They are impermanent. Desire is not what we are but it is the way we tend to react out of ignorance when we have not understood these Four Noble Truths in their three aspects. We tend to react like that to everything. These are normal reactions due to ignorance.

But we need not continue to suffer. We are not just hopeless victims of desire. We can allow desire to be the way it is and so begin to let go of it. Desire has power over us and deludes us only as long as we grasp it, believe in it and react to it.

GRASPING IS SUFFERING

Usually we equate suffering with feeling, but feeling is not suffering. It is the grasping of desire that is suffering. Desire does not cause suffering; the cause of suffering is the *grasping* of desire. This statement is for reflection and contemplation in terms of your individual experience.

You really have to investigate desire and know it for what it is. You have to know what is natural and necessary for survival and what is not necessary for survival. We can be very idealistic in thinking that even the need for food is some kind of desire we should not have. One can be quite ridiculous about it. But the Buddha was not an idealist and he was not a moralist. He was not trying to condemn anything. He was trying to awaken us to truth so that we could see things clearly.

Once there is that clarity and seeing in the right way, then there is no suffering. You can still feel hunger. You can still need food without it becoming a desire. Food is a natural need of the body. The body is not self; it needs food otherwise it will get very weak and die. That is the nature of the body – there is nothing wrong with that. If we get very moralistic and high-minded and believe that we *are* our bodies, that hunger is our own problem, and that we should not even eat – that is not wisdom; it is foolishness.

When you really see the origin of suffering, you realise that the problem is the grasping of desire not the desire itself. Grasping means being deluded by it, thinking it's really 'me' and 'mine': 'These desires are me and there is something wrong with me for having them'; or, 'I don't like the way I am now. I have to become something else'; or, 'I have to get rid of something before I can become what I want to be.' All this is desire. So you listen to it with bare attention not saying it's good or bad, but merely recognising it for what it is.

LETTING GO

If we contemplate desires and listen to them, we are actually no longer attaching to them; we are just allowing them to be the way they are. Then we come to the realisation that the origin of suffering, desire, can be laid aside and let go of.

How do you let go of things? This means you leave them as they are; it does not mean you annihilate them or throw them away. It is more like setting them down and letting them be. Through the practice of letting go we realise that there is

33

the origin of suffering, which is the attachment to desire, and we realise that we should let go of these three kinds of desire. Then we realise that we have let go of these desires; there is no longer any attachment to them.

When you find yourself attached, remember that 'letting go' is not 'getting rid of' or 'throwing away'. If I'm holding onto this clock and you say, 'Let go of it!', that doesn't mean 'throw it out'. I might think that I have to throw it away because I'm attached to it, but that would just be the desire to get rid of it. We tend to think that getting rid of the object is a way of getting rid of attachment. But if I can contemplate attachment, this grasping of the clock, I realise that there is no point in getting rid of it – it's a good clock; it keeps good time and is not heavy to carry around. The clock is not the problem. The problem is grasping the clock. So what do I do? Let it go, lay it aside – put it down gently without any kind of aversion. Then I can pick it up again, see what time it is and lay it aside when necessary.

You can apply this insight into 'letting go' to the desire for sense pleasures. Maybe you want to have a lot of fun. How would you lay aside that desire without any aversion? Simply recognise the desire without judging it. You can contemplate wanting to get rid of it – because you feel guilty about having such a foolish desire – but just lay it aside. Then, when you see it as it is, recognising that it's just desire, you are no longer attached to it.

So the way is always working with the moments of daily life. When you are feeling depressed and negative, just the moment that you refuse to indulge in that feeling is an enlightenment experience. When you see *that*, you need not sink into the sea of depression and despair and wallow in it. You can actually stop by learning not to give things a second thought.

You have to find this out through practice so that you will know for yourself how to let go of the origin of suffering. Can you let go of desire by wanting to let go of it? What is it that is really letting go in a given moment? You have to contem-

34

plate the experience of letting go and really examine and investigate until the insight comes. Keep with it until that insight comes: 'Ah, letting go, yes, now I understand. Desire is being let go of.' This does not mean that you are going to let go of desire forever but, at that one moment, you actually *have* let go and you have done it in full conscious awareness. There is an insight then. This is what we call insight knowledge. In Pali, we call it *ñanadassana* or profound understanding.

I had my first insight into letting go in my first year of meditation. I figured out intellectually that you had to let go of everything and then I thought: 'How do you let go?' It seemed impossible to let go of anything. I kept on contemplating: 'How do you let go?' Then I would say, 'You let go by letting go.' 'Well then, let go!' Then I would say: 'But have I let go yet?' and, 'How do you let go?' 'Well just let go!' I went on like that, getting more frustrated. But eventually it became obvious what was happening. If you try to analyse letting go in detail, you get caught up in making it very complicated. It was not something that you could figure out in words any more, but something you actually did. So I just let go for a moment, just like that.

Now with personal problems and obsessions, to let go of them is just that much. It is not a matter of analysing and endlessly making more of a problem about them, but of practising that state of leaving things alone, letting go of them. At first, you let go but then you pick them up again because the habit of grasping is so strong. But at least you have the idea. Even when I had that insight into letting go, I let go for a moment but then I started grasping by thinking: 'I can't do it, I have so many bad habits!' But don't trust that kind of nagging, disparaging thing in yourself. It is totally untrustworthy. It is just a matter of practising letting go. The more you begin to see how to do it, then the more you are able to sustain the state of non-attachment.

35

ACCOMPLISHMENT

It is important to know when you have let go of desire: when you no longer judge or try to get rid of it; when you recognise that it's just the way it is. When you are really calm and peaceful, then you will find that there is no attachment to anything. You are not caught up, trying to get something or trying to get rid of something. Well-being is just knowing things as they are without feeling the necessity to pass judgment upon them.

We say all the time, 'This shouldn't be like this!', 'I shouldn't be this way!' and, 'You shouldn't be like this and you shouldn't do that!', and so on. I'm sure I could tell you what you should be – and you could tell me what I should be. We should be kind, loving, generous, good-hearted, hard-working, diligent, courageous, brave and compassionate. I don't have to know you at all to tell you that! But to really know you, I would have to open up to you rather than start from an ideal about what a woman or man should be, what a Buddhist should be or what a Christian should be. It's not that we don't know what we should be.

Our suffering comes from the attachment that we have to ideals, and the complexities we create about the way things are. We are never what we should be according to our highest ideals. Life, others, the country we are in, the world we live in – things never seem to be what they should be. We become very critical of everything and of ourselves: 'I know I should be more patient, but I just CAN'T be patient!' . . . Listen to all the 'shoulds' and the 'should nots' and the desires: wanting the pleasant, wanting to become or wanting to get rid of the ugly and the painful. It's like listening to somebody talking over the fence saying, 'I want this and I don't like that. It should be this way and it shouldn't be that way.' Really take time to listen to the complaining mind; bring it into consciousness.

I used to do a lot of this when I felt discontented or critical. I would close my eyes and start thinking, 'I don't like this and

I don't want that', 'That person shouldn't be like this', and 'The world shouldn't be like that.' I would keep listening to this kind of critical demon that would go on and on, criticising me, you and the world. Then I would think, 'I want happiness and comfort; I want to feel safe; I want to be loved!' I would deliberately think these things out and listen to them in order to know them simply as conditions that arise in the mind. So bring them up in *your* mind – arouse all the hopes, desires and criticisms. Bring them into consciousness. Then you will know desire and be able to lay it aside.

The more we contemplate and investigate grasping, the more the insight arises: 'Desire should be let go of.' Then, through the actual practice and understanding of what letting go really is, we have the third insight into the Second Noble Truth, which is: 'Desire has been let go of.' We actually know letting go. It is not a theoretical letting go, but a direct insight. You know letting go has been accomplished. This is what practice is all about.

THE THIRD NOBLE
TRUTH

What is the Noble Truth of the Cessation of Suffering?
It is the remainderless fading and cessation of that same
craving; the rejecting, relinquishing, leaving and renouncing
of it. But whereon is this craving abandoned and made to
cease? Wherever there is what seems lovable and gratifying,
thereon it is abandoned and made to cease.
There is this Noble Truth of the Cessation of Suffering: such
was the vision, insight, wisdom, knowing and light that arose
in me about things not heard before.
This Noble Truth must be penetrated to by realising
the Cessation of Suffering. . . .
This Noble Truth has been penetrated to by realising the
Cessation of Suffering: such was the vision, insight,
wisdom, knowing and light that arose in me about things
not heard before. [Samyutta Nikaya LVI, 11]

The Third Noble Truth with its three aspects is: 'There
is the cessation of suffering, of *dukkha*. The cessation
of *dukkha* should be realised. The cessation of *dukkha* has been
realised.'

The whole aim of the Buddhist teaching is to develop the
reflective mind in order to let go of delusions. The Four Noble
Truths is a teaching about letting go by investigating or looking
into – contemplating: 'Why is it like this? Why is it this way?'

It is good to ponder over things like why monks shave their heads or why Buddha-rupas* look the way they do. We contemplate . . . the mind is not forming an opinion about whether these are good, bad, useful or useless. The mind is actually opening and considering, 'What does this mean? What do the monks represent? Why do they carry alms bowls? Why can't they have money? Why can't they grow their own food?' We contemplate how this way of living has sustained the tradition and allowed it to be handed down from its original founder, Gotama the Buddha, to the present time.

We reflect as we see suffering; as we see the nature of desire; as we recognise that attachment to desire is suffering. Then we have the insight of allowing desire to go and the realisation of non-suffering, the cessation of suffering. These insights can only come through reflection; they cannot come through belief. You cannot make yourself believe or realise an insight as a wilful act; through really contemplating and pondering these truths, the insights come to you. They come only through the mind being open and receptive to the teaching – blind belief is certainly not advised or expected of anyone. Instead, the mind should be willing to be receptive, pondering and considering.

This mental state is very important – it is the way out of suffering. It is not the mind which has fixed views and prejudices and thinks it knows it all or which just takes what other people say as being the truth. It is the mind that is open to these Four Noble Truths and can reflect upon something that we can see within our own mind.

People rarely realise non-suffering because it takes a special kind of willingness in order to ponder and investigate and get beyond the gross and the obvious. It takes a willingness to actually look at your own reactions, to be able to see the attachments and to contemplate: 'What does attachment feel like?'

For example, do you feel happy or liberated by being attached to desire? Is it uplifting or depressing? These

39

questions are for you to investigate. If you find out that being attached to your desires is liberating, then do that. Attach to all your desires and see what the result is.

In my practice, I have seen that attachment to my desires is suffering. There is no doubt about that. I can see how much suffering in my life has been caused by attachments to material things, ideas, attitudes or fears. I can see all kinds of unnecessary misery that I have caused myself through attachment because I did not know any better. I was brought up in America – the land of freedom. It promises the right to be happy, but what it really offers is the right to be attached to everything. America encourages you to try to be as happy as you can by getting things. However, if you are working with the Four Noble Truths, attachment is to be understood and contemplated; then the insight into non-attachment arises. This , not an intellectual stand or a command from your brain saying that you should not be attached; it is just a natural insight into non-attachment or non-suffering.

THE TRUTH OF IMPERMANENCE

Here at Amaravati, we chant the Dhammacakkappavattana Sutta in its traditional form. When the Buddha gave this sermon on the Four Noble Truths, only one of the five disciples who listened to it really understood it; only one had the profound insight. The other four rather liked it, thinking 'Very nice teaching indeed,' but only one of the them, Kondañña, really had the perfect understanding of what the Buddha was saying.

The devas were also listening to the sermon. Devas are celestial, ethereal creatures, vastly superior to us. They do not have coarse bodies like ours; they have ethereal bodies and they are beautiful and lovely, intelligent. Now although they were delighted to hear the sermon, not one of them was enlightened by it.

We are told that they became very happy about the Buddha's enlightenment and that they shouted up through the

40

heavens when they heard his teaching. First, one level of *devata* heard it, then they shouted up to the next level and soon all the *devas* were rejoicing – right up to the highest, the *Brahma* realm. There was resounding joy that the Wheel of Dhamma was set rolling and these *devas* and *brahmas* were rejoicing in it. However, only Kondañña, one of the five disciples, was enlightened when he heard this sermon. At the very end of the sutta, the Buddha called him 'Añña Kondañña'. 'Añña' means profound knowing, so 'Añña Kondañña' means 'Kondañña-Who-Knows.'

What did Kondañña know? What was his insight that the Buddha praised at the very end of the sermon? It was: 'All that is subject to arising is subject to ceasing.' Now this may not sound like any great knowledge but what it really implies is a universal pattern: whatever is subject to arising is subject to ceasing; it is impermanent and not self. . . . So don't attach, don't be deluded by what arises and ceases. Don't look for your refuges, that which you want to abide in and trust, in anything that arises – because those things will cease.

If you want to suffer and waste your life, go around seeking things that arise. They will all take you to the end, to cessation, and you will not be any the wiser for it. You will just go around repeating the same old dreary habits and when you die, you will not have learned anything important from your life.

Rather than just thinking about it, really contemplate: 'All that is subject to arising is subject to ceasing.' Apply it to life in general, to your own experience. Then you will understand. Just note: beginning . . . ending. Contemplate how things are. This sensory realm is all about arising and ceasing, beginning and ending; there can be perfect understanding, *samma ditthi*, in this lifetime. I don't know how long Kondañña lived after the Buddha's sermon, but he was enlightened at that moment. Right then, he had perfect understanding.

I would like to emphasise how important it is to develop this way of reflecting. Rather than just developing a method of tranquillising your mind, which certainly is one part of the

41

practice, really see that proper meditation is a commitment to wise investigation. It involves a courageous effort to look deeply into things, not analysing yourself and making judgments about why you suffer on a personal level, but resolving to really follow the path until you have profound understanding. Such perfect understanding is based upon the pattern of arising and ceasing. Once this law is understood, everything is seen as fitting into that pattern.

This is not a metaphysical teaching: 'All that is subject to arising is subject to ceasing.' It is not about the ultimate reality – the deathless reality; but if you profoundly understand and know that all that is subject to arising is subject to ceasing, then you will *realise* the ultimate reality, the deathless, immortal truths. This is a skilful means to that ultimate realisation. Notice the difference: the statement is not a metaphysical one but one which takes us to metaphysical realisation.

MORTALiTY AND CESSATION

With the reflection upon the Noble Truths, we bring into consciousness this very problem of human existence. We look at this sense of alienation and blind attachment to sensory consciousness, the attachment to that which is separate and stands forth in consciousness. Out of ignorance, we attach to desires for sense pleasures. When we identify with what is mortal or death-bound, and with what is unsatisfactory, that very attachment is suffering.

Sense pleasures are all mortal pleasures. Whatever we see, hear, touch, taste, think or feel is mortal – death-bound. So when we attach to the mortal senses, we attach to death. If we have not contemplated or understood it, we just attach blindly to mortality hoping that we can stave it off for a while. We pretend that we're going to be really happy with the things we attach to – only to feel eventually disillusioned, despairing and disappointed. We might succeed in becoming what we want, but that too is mortal. We're attaching to another death-bound condition. Then, with the desire to die, we might attach to

42

suicide or to annihilation – but death itself is yet another death-bound condition. Whatever we attach to in these three kinds of desires, we're attaching to death – which means that we're going to experience disappointment or despair.

Death of the mind is despair; depression is a kind of death experience of the mind. Just as the body dies a physical death, the mind dies. Mental states and mental conditions die; we call it despair, boredom, depression and anguish. Whenever we attach, if we're experiencing boredom, despair, anguish and sorrow, we tend to seek some other mortal condition that's arising. As an example, you feel despair and you think, 'I want a piece of chocolate cake.' Off you go! For a moment you can absorb into the sweet, delicious, chocolate flavour of that piece of cake. At that moment, there's becoming – you've actually become the sweet, delicious, chocolate flavour! But you can't hold on to that very long. You swallow and what's left? Then you have to go on to do something else. This is 'becoming'.

We are blinded, caught in this becoming process on the sensual plane. But through knowing desire without judging the beauty or ugliness of the sensual plane, we come to see desire as it is. There's knowing. Then, by laying aside these desires rather than grasping at them, we experience *nirodha*, the cessation of suffering. This is the Third Noble Truth which we must realise for ourselves. We contemplate cessation. We say, 'There is cessation', and we know when something has ceased.

ALLOWING THINGS TO ARISE

Before you can let things go, you have to admit them into full consciousness. In meditation, our aim is to skilfully allow the subconscious to arise into consciousness. All the despair, fears, anguish, suppression and anger is allowed to become conscious. There is a tendency in people to hold to very high-minded ideals. We can become very disappointed in ourselves because sometimes we feel we are not as good as we should be or we should not feel angry – all the shoulds and shouldn'ts. Then we create desire to get rid of the bad things – and this desire has a righteous quality. It seems right to get rid of bad thoughts, anger and jealousy because a good person 'should not be like that'. Thus, we create guilt.

In reflecting on this, we bring into consciousness the desire to become this ideal and the desire to get rid of these bad things. And by doing that, we can let go – so that rather than becoming the perfect person, you let go of that desire. What is left is the pure mind. There is no need to become the perfect person because the pure mind is where perfect people arise and cease.

Cessation is easy to understand on an intellectual level, but to *realise* it may be quite difficult because this entails abiding with what we think we cannot bear. For example, when I first started meditating, I had the idea that meditation would make me kinder and happier and I was expecting to experience blissful mind states. But during the first two months, I never felt so much hatred and anger in my life. I thought, 'This is terrible; meditation has made me worse.' But then I contemplated why was there so much hatred and aversion coming up, and I realised that much of my life had been an attempt to run away from all that. I used to be a compulsive reader. I would have to take books with me where-ever I went. Anytime fear or aversion started creeping in, I would whip out my book and read; or I would smoke or munch on snacks. I had an image of myself as being a kind person that did not hate people, so any hint of aversion or hatred was repressed.

This is why during the first few months as a monk, I was so desperate for things to do. I was trying to seek something to distract myself with because I had started to remember in meditation all the things I deliberately tried to forget. Memories from childhood and adolescence kept coming up in my mind; then this anger and hatred became so conscious it just seemed to overwhelm me. But something in me began to recognise that I had to bear with this, so I did stick it out. All the hatred and anger that had been suppressed in thirty years of living rose to its peak at this time, and it burned itself out and ceased through meditation. It was a process of purification.

To allow this process of cessation to work, we must be willing to suffer. This is why I stress the importance of patience. We have to open our minds to suffering because it is in embracing suffering that suffering ceases. When we find that we are suffering, physically or mentally, then we go to the actual suffering that is present. We open completely to it, welcome it, concentrate on it, allowing it to be what it is. That means we must be patient and bear with the unpleasantness of a particular condition. We have to endure boredom, despair, doubt and fear in order to understand that they cease rather than running away from them.

As long as we do not allow things to cease, we just create new *kamma* that just reinforces our habits. When something arises, we grasp it and proliferate around it; and this complicates everything. Then these things will be repeated and repeated throughout our lives – we cannot go around following our desires and fears and expect to realise peace. We contemplate fear and desire so that these do not delude us anymore: we have to know what is deluding us before we can let it go. Desire and fear are to be known as impermanent, unsatisfactory and not-self. They are seen and penetrated so that suffering can burn itself away.

It is very important here to differentiate between *cessation* and *annihilation* – the desire that comes into the mind to get rid of something. Cessation is the natural ending of any condition that has arisen. So it is not desire! It is not something that we create in the mind but it is the end of that which began, the death of that which is born. Therefore, cessation is not a self – it does not come about from a sense of 'I have to get rid of things,' but when we allow that which has arisen to cease. To do that, one has to abandon craving – let it go. It does not mean rejecting or throwing away but abandoning means letting go of it.

Then, when it has ceased, you experience *nirodha* – cessation, emptiness, non-attachment. *Nirodha* is another word for Nibbana. When you have let something go and allowed it to cease, then what is left is peace.

You can experience that peace through your own meditation. When you've let desire end in your own mind, that which is left over is very peaceful. That is true peacefulness, the Deathless. When you really know that as it is, you realise *nirodha sacca*, the Truth of Cessation, in which there's no self but there's still alertness and clarity. The real meaning of bliss is that peaceful, transcendent consciousness.

If we do not allow cessation, then we tend to operate from assumptions we make about ourselves without even knowing what we are doing. Sometimes, it is not until we start meditating that we begin to realise how in our lives so much fear and lack of confidence come from childhood experiences. I remember when I was a little boy, I had a very good friend who turned on me and rejected me. I was distraught for months after that. It left an indelible impression on my mind. Then I realised through meditation just how much a little incident like that had affected my future relationships with others – I always had a tremendous fear of rejection. I never even thought of it until that particular memory kept rising up into my consciousness during meditation. The rational mind knows that it is ridiculous to go around thinking about the tragedies of childhood. But if they keep coming up into consciousness when you are middle-aged, maybe they are trying to tell you something about assumptions that were formed when you were a child.

When you begin to feel memories or obsessive fears coming up in meditation, rather than becoming frustrated or upset by them, see them as something to be accepted into consciousness so that you can let them go. You can arrange your daily life so that you never have to look at these things; then the conditions for them to actually arise are minimal. You can dedicate yourself to a lot of important causes and keep busy;

then these anxieties and nameless fears never become conscious – but what happens when you let go? The desire or obsession moves – and it moves to cessation. It ends. And then you have the insight that there is the cessation of desire. So the third aspect of the Third Noble Truth is: cessation has been realised.

REALISATION

This is to be realised. The Buddha said emphatically: 'This is a Truth to be realised here and now.' We do not have to wait until we die to find out if it's all true – this teaching is for living human beings like ourselves. Each one of us has to realise it. I may tell you about it and encourage you to do it but I can't make you realise it!

Don't think of it as something remote or beyond your ability. When we talk about Dhamma or Truth, we say that it is here and now, and something we can see for ourselves. We can turn to it; we can incline towards the Truth. We can pay attention to the way it is, here and now, at this time and this place. That's mindfulness – being alert and bringing attention to the way it is. Through mindfulness, we investigate the sense of self, this sense of me and mine: my body, my feelings, my memories, my thoughts, my views, my opinions, my house, my car and so on.

My tendency was self-disparagement so, for example, with the thought: 'I am Sumedho,' I'd think of myself in negative terms: 'I'm no good.' But listen, from where does that arise and where does it cease? . . . or, 'I'm really better than you, I'm more highly attained. I've been living the Holy Life for a long time so I must be better than any of you!' Where does THAT arise and cease?

When there is arrogance, conceit or self disparagement – whatever it is – examine it; listen inwardly: 'I am. . . .' Be aware and attentive to the space before you think it; then think it and notice the space that follows. Sustain your attention on that emptiness at the end and see how long you can hold your

47

attention on it. See if you can hear a kind of ringing sound in the mind, the sound of silence, the primordial sound. When you concentrate your attention on that, you can reflect: 'Is there any sense of self?' You see that when you're really empty – when there's just clarity, alertness and attention – there's no self. There's no sense of me and mine. So, I go to that empty state and I contemplate Dhamma: I think, 'This is just as it is. This body here is just this way.' I can give it a name or not but right now, it's just this way. It's not Sumedho!

There's no Buddhist monk in the emptiness. 'Buddhist monk' is merely a convention, appropriate to time and place. When people praise you and say, 'How wonderful', you can know it as someone giving praise without taking it personally. You know there's no Buddhist monk there; it's just Suchness. It's just this way. If I want Amaravati to be a successful place and it is a great success, I'm happy. But if it all fails, if no one is interested, we can't pay the electricity bill and everything falls apart – failure! But really, there's no Amaravati. The idea of a person who is a Buddhist monk or a place called Amaravati – these are only conventions, not ultimate realities. Right now it's just this way, just the way it's supposed to be. One doesn't carry the burden of such a place on one's shoulders because one sees it as it really is and there's no person to be involved in it. Whether it succeeds or fails is no longer important in the same way.

In emptiness, things are just what they are. When we are aware in this way, it doesn't mean that we are indifferent to success or failure and that we don't bother to do anything. We can apply ourselves. We know what we can do; we know what has to be done and we can do it in the right way. Then everything becomes Dhamma, the way it is. We do things because that is the right thing to be doing at this time and in this place rather than out of a sense of personal ambition or fear of failure.

The path to the cessation of suffering is the path of perfection. Perfection can be a rather daunting word because

48

we feel very imperfect. As personalities, we wonder how we can dare to even entertain the possibility of being perfect. Human perfection is something no one ever talks about; it doesn't seem at all possible to think of perfection in regard to being human. But an arahant is simply a human being who has perfected life, someone who has learned everything there is to learn through the basic law: 'All that is subject to arising is subject to ceasing.' An arahant does not need to know everything about everything; it is only necessary to know and fully understand this law.

We use Buddha wisdom to contemplate Dhamma, the way things are. We take Refuge in Sangha, in that which is doing good and refraining from doing evil. Sangha is one thing, a community. It's not a group of individual personalities or different characters. The sense of being an individual person or a man or a woman is no longer important to us. This sense of Sangha is realised as a Refuge. There is that unity so that even though the manifestations are all individual, our realisation is the same. Through being awake, alert and no longer attached, we realise cessation and we abide in emptiness where we all merge. There's no person there. People may arise and cease in the emptiness, but there's no person. There's just clarity, awareness, peacefulness and purity.

THE FOURTH NOBLE TRUTH

What is the Noble Truth of the Way Leading to the Cessation
of Suffering? It is this Noble Eightfold Path, that is to say:
Right View, Right Intention, Right Speech, Right Action,
Right Livelihood, Right Effort, Right Mindfulness and
Right Concentration.
There is this Noble Truth of the Path leading to the Cessation
of Suffering: such was the vision, insight, wisdom, knowing
and light that arose in me about things not heard before. . . .
This Noble Truth must be penetrated to by cultivating
the Path. . . .
This Noble Truth has been penetrated to by cultivating the Path:
such was the vision, insight, wisdom, knowing and light that
arose in me about things not heard before.
[Samyutta Nikaya LVI, 11]

The Fourth Noble Truth, like the first three, has three
aspects. The first aspect is: 'There is the Eightfold
Path, the *atthangika magga* – the way out of suffering.' It is also
called the *ariya magga*, the Ariyan or Noble Path. The second
aspect is: 'This path should be developed.' The final insight
into arahantship is: 'This path has been fully developed.'

The Eightfold Path is presented in a sequence: beginning
with Right (or perfect) Understanding, *samma ditthi*, it goes to
Right (or perfect) Intention or Aspiration, *samma sankappa;*

these first two elements of the path are grouped together as Wisdom (*pañña*). Moral commitment (*sila*) flows from *pañña*; this covers Right Speech, Right Action and Right Livelihood – also referred to as perfect speech, perfect action and perfect livelihood, *samma vaca, samma kammanta* and *samma ajiva*.

Then we have Right Effort, Right Mindfulness and Right Concentration, *samma vayama, samma sati* and *samma samadhi*, which flow naturally from *sila*. These last three provide emotional balance. They are about the heart – the heart that is liberated from self-view and from selfishness. With Right Effort, Right Mindfulness and Right Concentration, the heart is pure, free from taints and defilements. When the heart is pure, the mind is peaceful. Wisdom (*pañña*), or Right Understanding and Right Aspiration, comes from a pure heart. This takes us back to where we started.

These, then, are the elements of the Eightfold Path, grouped in three sections:

1. Wisdom (*pañña*)
   Right Understanding (*samma ditthi*)
   Right Aspiration (*samma sankappa*)
2. Morality (*sila*)
   Right Speech (*samma vaca*)
   Right Action (*samma kammanta*)
   Right Livelihood (*samma ajiva*)
3. Concentration (*samadhi*)
   Right Effort (*samma vayama*)
   Right Mindfulness (*samma sati*)
   Right Concentration (*samma samadhi*)

The fact that we list them in order does not mean that they happen in a linear way, in sequence – they arise together. We may talk about the Eightfold Path and say 'First you have Right Understanding, then you have Right Aspiration, then . . . .' But actually, presented in this way, it simply teaches us to reflect upon the importance of taking responsibility for what we say and do in our lives.

RIGHT UNDERSTANDING

The first element of the Eightfold Path is Right Understanding which arises through insights into the first three Noble Truths. If you have those insights, then there is perfect understanding of Dhamma – the understanding that: 'All that is subject to arising is subject to ceasing.' It's as simple as that. You do not have to spend much time reading 'All that is subject to arising is subject to ceasing' to understand the words, but it takes quite a while for most of us to really know what the words mean in a profound way rather than just through cerebral understanding.

To use modern colloquial English, insight is really gut knowledge – it's not just from ideas. It's no longer, 'I *think* I know', or 'Oh yes, that seems a reasonable, sensible thing. I agree with that. I like that thought.' That kind of understanding is still from the brain whereas insight knowledge is profound. It is really known and doubt is no longer a problem.

This deep understanding comes from the previous nine insights. So there is a sequence leading to Right Understanding of things as they are, namely that: All that is subject to arising is subject to ceasing and is not-self. With Right Understanding, you have given up the illusion of a self that is connected to mortal conditions. There is still the body, there are still feelings and thoughts, but they simply are what they are – there is no longer the belief that you *are* your body or your feelings or your thoughts. The emphasis is on 'Things are what they are.' We are not trying to say that things are not anything at all or that they are not what they are. They are exactly what they are and nothing more. But when we are ignorant, when we have not understood these truths, we tend to think things are more than what they are. We believe all kinds of things and we create all kinds of problems around the conditions that we experience.

So much of human anguish and despair comes from the added extra that is born of ignorance in the moment. It is sad to realise how the misery and anguish and despair of humanity is based upon delusion; the despair is empty and meaningless. When you see this, you begin to feel infinite compassion for all beings. How can you hate anyone or bear grudges or condemn anyone who is caught in this bond of ignorance? Everyone is influenced to do the things they do by their wrong views of things.

As we meditate, we experience some tranquillity, a measure of calm in which the mind has slowed down. When we look at something like a flower with a calm mind, we are looking at it as it is. When there is no grasping – nothing to gain or get rid of – then if what we see, hear or experience through the senses is beautiful, it is truly beautiful. We are not criticising it, comparing it, trying to possess or own it; we find delight and joy in the beauty around us because there is no need to make anything out of it. It is exactly what it is.

Beauty reminds us of purity, truth and ultimate beauty. We should not see it as a lure to delude us: 'These flowers are here just to attract me so I'll get deluded by them' – that's the attitude of the old meditating grump! When we look at a member of the opposite sex with a pure heart, we appreciate the beauty without desire for some kind of contact or possession. We can delight in the beauty of other people, both men and women, when there is no selfish interest or desire. There is honesty; things are what they are. This is what we mean by liberation or *vimutti* in Pali. We are liberated from those bonds that distort and corrupt the beauty around us, such as the bodies we have. However, our minds can get so corrupt and negative and depressed and obsessed with things, that we no longer see them as they are. If we don't have Right Understanding, we see everything through increasingly thick filters and veils.

Right Understanding is to be developed through reflection, using the Buddha's teaching. The Dhammacakkappavattana Sutta itself is a very interesting teaching to contemplate and use as a reference for reflection. We can also use other suttas from the *tipitaka**, such as the those dealing with *paticcasamuppada* (dependent origination*). This is a fascinating teaching to reflect upon. If you can contemplate such teachings, you can see very clearly the difference between the way things are as Dhamma and the point where we tend to create delusion out of the way things are. That is why we need to establish full conscious awareness of things as they are. If there is knowledge of the Four Noble Truths, then there is Dhamma.

With Right Understanding, everything is seen as Dhamma; for example: we are sitting here. . . . This is Dhamma. We don't think of this body and mind as a personality with all its views and opinions and all the conditioned thoughts and reactions that we have acquired through ignorance. We reflect upon this moment now as: 'This is the way it is. This is Dhamma.' We bring into the mind the understanding that this physical formation is simply Dhamma. It is not self; it is not personal.

Also, we see the sensitivity of this physical formation as Dhamma rather than taking it personally: 'I'm sensitive,' or 'I'm not sensitive;' 'You're not sensitive to me. Who's the most sensitive?' . . . 'Why do we feel pain? Why did God create pain; why didn't he just create pleasure? Why is there so much misery and suffering in the world? It's unfair. People die and we have to separate from the people we love; the anguish is terrible.'

There is no Dhamma in that, is there? It's all self-view: 'Poor me. I don't like this, I don't want it to be this way. I want security, happiness, pleasure and all the best of everything; it's not fair that I don't have these things. It's not fair that my parents were not arahants when I came into the world. It's not fair that they never elect arahants to be Prime Minister of Britain. If everything were fair, they would elect arahants to be Prime Minister!'

I am trying to take this sense of 'It's not right, it's not fair' to an absurdity in order to point out how we expect God to create everything for us and to make us happy and secure. That is often what people think even if they don't say so. But when we reflect, we see 'This is the way it is. Pain is like this and this is what pleasure is like. Consciousness is this way.' We feel. We breathe. We can aspire.

When we reflect, we contemplate our own humanity as it is. We don't take it on a personal level any more or blame anyone because things are not exactly as we like or want. It is the way it is and we are the way we are. You might ask why we can't all be exactly the same – with the same anger, the same greed and the same ignorance; without all the variations and permutations. However, even though you can trace human experience to basic things, each one of us has our own *kamma** to deal with – our own obsessions and tendencies, which are always different in quality and quantity to those of someone else.

Why can't we all be exactly equal, have exactly the same of everything and all look alike – one androgynous being? In a world like that, nothing would be unfair, no differences would be allowed, everything would be absolutely perfect and there would be no possibility of inequality. But as we recognise Dhamma, we see that, within the realm of conditions, no two things are identical. They are all quite different, infinitely variable and changing, and the more we try to make conditions conform to our ideas, the more frustrated we get. We try to create each other and a society to fit the ideas we have of how things should be, but we always end up feeling frustrated. With reflection, we realise: 'This is the way it is,' this is the way things have to be – they can only be this way.

Now that is not a fatalistic or negative reflection. It is not an attitude of: 'That's the way it is and there's nothing you can do about it.' It is a very positive response of accepting the flow of life for what it is. Even if it is not what we want, we can accept it and learn from it.

✧ ✧ ✧

We are conscious, intelligent beings with retentive memory. We have language. Over the past several thousand years, we have developed reason, logic and discriminative intelligence. What we must do is figure out how to use these capacities as tools for realisation of Dhamma rather than as personal acquisitions or personal problems. People who develop their discriminative intelligence often end up turning it upon themselves; they become very self-critical and even begin to hate themselves. This is because our discriminative faculties tend to focus upon what is wrong with everything. That is what discrimination is about: seeing how *this* is different from *that*. When you do that to yourself, what do you end up with? Just a whole list of flaws and faults that make you sound absolutely hopeless.

When we are developing Right Understanding, we use our intelligence for reflection and contemplation of things. We also use our mindfulness, being open to the way it is. When we reflect in this way, we are using mindfulness and wisdom together. So now we are using our ability to discriminate with wisdom (*vijja*) rather than with ignorance (*avijja*). This teaching of the Four Noble Truths is to help you to use your intelligence – your ability to contemplate, reflect and think – in a wise way rather than in a self-destructive, greedy or hateful way.

RIGHT ASPIRATION

The second element of the Eightfold Path is *samma sankappa*. Sometimes this is translated as 'Right Thought', thinking in the right way. However, it actually has more of a dynamic quality – like 'intention', 'attitude' or 'aspiration'. I like to use 'aspiration' which is somehow very meaningful in this Eightfold Path – because we do aspire.

It is important to see that aspiration is not desire. The Pali word '*tanha*' means desire that comes out of ignorance, whereas '*sankappa*' means aspiration not coming from ignorance. Aspiration might seem like a kind of desire to us because in

English we use the word 'desire' for everything of that nature – either aspiring or wanting. You might think that aspiration is a kind of *tanha*, wanting to *become* enlightened (*bhava tanha*) – but *samma sankappa* comes from Right Understanding, seeing clearly. It is not wanting to become anything; it is not the desire to become an enlightened person. With Right Understanding, that whole illusion and way of thinking no longer makes sense.

Aspiration is a feeling, intention, attitude or movement within us. Our spirit rises, it does not sink downwards – it is not desperation! When there is Right Understanding, we aspire to truth, beauty and goodness. *Samma ditthi* and *samma sankappa*, Right Understanding and Right Aspiration, are called *pañña* or wisdom and they make up the first of the three sections in the Eightfold Path.

We can contemplate: Why is it that we still feel discontented, even when we have the best of everything? We are not completely happy even if we have a beautiful house, a car, the perfect marriage, lovely bright children and all the rest of it – and we are certainly not contented when we do not have all these things! . . . If we don't have them, we can think, 'Well, if I had the best, *then* I'd be content.' But we wouldn't be. The earth is not the place for our contentment; it's not supposed to be. When we realise that, we no longer expect contentment from planet earth; we do not make that demand.

Until we realise that this planet cannot satisfy all our wants, we keep on asking, 'Why can't you make me content, Mother Earth?' We are like little children who suckle their mother, constantly trying to get the most out of her and wanting her always to nurture and feed them and make them feel content.

If we were content, we would not wonder about things. Yet we do recognise that there is something more than just the ground under our feet; there is something above us that we cannot quite understand. We have the ability to wonder and ponder about life, to contemplate its meaning. If you want to know the meaning of your life, you cannot be content with material wealth, comfort and security alone.

So we aspire to know the truth. You might think that that is a kind of presumptuous desire or aspiration, 'Who do I think I am? Little old me trying to know the truth about everything.' But there is that aspiration. Why do we have it if it is not possible? Consider the concept of ultimate reality. An absolute or ultimate truth is a very refined concept; the idea of God, the Deathless or the immortal, is actually a very refined thought. We aspire to know that ultimate reality. The animal side of us does not aspire; it does not know anything about such aspirations. But there is in each of us an intuitive intelligence that wants to know; it is always with us but we tend to not notice it; we do not understand it. We tend to discard or mistrust it – especially modern materialists. They just think it is fantasy and not real.

As for myself, I was really happy when I realised that the planet is not my real home. I had always suspected it. I can remember even as a small child thinking, 'I don't really belong here.' I have never particularly felt that planet Earth is where I really belong – even before I was a monk, I never felt that I fitted into the society. For some people, that could be just a neurotic problem, but perhaps it could also be the kind of intuition children often have. When you are innocent, your mind is very intuitive. The mind of a child is more intuitively in touch with mysterious forces than most adult minds are. As we grow up we become conditioned to think in very set ways and to have fixed ideas about what is real and what is not. As we develop our egos, society dictates what is real and what is not, what is right and what is wrong, and we begin to interpret the world through those fixed perceptions. One thing we find charming in children is that they don't do that yet; they still see the world with the intuitive mind that is not yet conditioned.

Meditation is a way of deconditioning the mind which helps us to let go of all the hard-line views and fixed ideas we have. Ordinarily, what is real is dismissed while what is not real is given all our attention. This is what ignorance (*avijja*) is.

The contemplation of our human aspiration connects us to something higher than just the animal kingdom or the planet earth. To me that connection seems more true than the idea that this is all there is; that once we die our bodies rot and there is nothing more than that. When we ponder and wonder about this universe we are living in, we see that it is very vast, mysterious and incomprehensible to us. However, when we trust more in our intuitive mind, we can be receptive to things that we may have forgotten or have never been open to before – we open when we let go of fixed, conditioned reactions.

We can have the fixed idea of being a personality, of being a man or a woman, being an English person or an American. These things can be very real to us, and we can get very upset and angry about them. We are even willing to kill each other over these conditioned views that we hold and believe in and never question. Without Right Aspiration and Right Understanding, without *pañña*, we never see the true nature of these views.

RIGHT SPEECH, RIGHT ACTION, RIGHT LIVELIHOOD

Sila, the moral aspect of the Eightfold Path, consists of Right Speech, Right Action and Right Livelihood; that means taking responsibility for our speech and being careful about what we do with our bodies. When I'm mindful and aware, I speak in a way that is appropriate to time and place; likewise, I act or work according to time and place.

We begin to realise that we have to be careful about what we do and say; otherwise we constantly hurt ourselves. If you do or say things that are unkind or cruel there is always an immediate result. In the past, you might have been able to get away with lying by distracting yourself, going on to something else so that you didn't have to think about it. You could forget all about things for a while until eventually they'd come back upon you, but if we practise *sila*, things seem to come back right away. Even when I exaggerate, something in me says, 'You shouldn't exaggerate, you should be more careful.' I used to have the habit of exaggerating things – it's part of our culture; it seems perfectly normal. But when you are aware, the effect of even the slightest lie or gossip is immediate because you are completely open, vulnerable and sensitive. So then you are careful about what you do; you realise that it's important to be responsible for what you do and say.

The impulse to help someone is a skilful *dhamma**. If you see someone fall over on the floor in a faint, a skilful *dhamma* goes through your mind: 'Help this person,' and you go to help them recover from their fainting spell. If you do it with an empty mind – not out of any personal desire for gain, but just out of compassion and because it's the right thing to do – then it's simply a skilful *dhamma*. It's not personal *kamma*; it's not yours. But if you do it out of a desire to gain merit and to impress other people or because the person is rich and you expect some reward for your action, then – even though the action is skilful – you're making a personal connection to it, and this reinforces the sense of self. When we do good works out of mindfulness and wisdom rather than out of ignorance, they are skilful *dhammas* without personal *kamma*.

The monastic order was established by the Buddha so that men and women could live an impeccable life which is completely blameless. As a bhikkhu, you live within a whole system of training precepts called the *Patimokkha* discipline. When you live under this discipline, even if your actions or speech are heedless, at least they don't leave strong impressions. You can't have money so you're not able to just go anywhere until you're invited. You are celibate. Since you live on almsfood, you're not killing any animals. You don't even pick flowers or leaves or do any kind of action that would disturb the natural flow in any way; you're completely harmless. In fact, in Thai-

60

land we had to carry water strainers with us to filter out any kind of living things in the water such as mosquito larvae. It's totally forbidden to intentionally kill things.

I have been living under this Rule for twenty-five years now so I haven't really done any heavy kammic actions. Under this discipline, one lives in a very harmless, very responsible way. Perhaps the most difficult part is with speech; speech habits are the most difficult to break and let go of – but they can also improve. By reflection and contemplation, one begins to see the unpleasantness of saying foolish things or just babbling or chatting away for no good reason.

For lay people, Right Livelihood is something that is developed as you come to know your intentions for what you do. You can try to avoid deliberately harming other creatures or earning a living in a harmful, unkind way. You can also try to avoid livelihood which may cause other people to become addicted to drugs or drink or which might endanger the ecological balance of the planet.

So these three – Right Action, Right Speech and Right Livelihood – follow from Right Understanding or perfect knowing. We begin to feel that we want to live in a way that is a blessing to this planet or, at least, that does not harm it.

Right Understanding and Right Aspiration have a definite influence on what we do and say. So *pañña*, or wisdom, leads to *sila*: Right Speech, Right Action and Right Livelihood. *Sila* refers to our speech and actions; with *sila* we contain the sexual drive or the violent use of the body – we do not use it for killing or stealing. In this way, *pañña* and *sila* work together in perfect harmony.

RIGHT EFFORT, RIGHT MINDFULNESS, RIGHT CONCENTRATION

Right Effort, Right Mindfulness and Right Concentration refer to your spirit, your heart. When we think of the spirit, we point to the centre of the chest, to the heart. So we have *pañña* (the head), *sila* (the body) and *samadhi* (the heart). You can use your own body as a kind of chart, a symbol of the Eightfold Path. These three are integrated, working together for realisation and supporting each other like a tripod. One is not dominating the other and exploiting or rejecting anything.

They work together: the wisdom from Right Understanding and Right Intention; then morality, which is Right Speech, Right Action and Right Livelihood; and Right Effort, Right Mindfulness and Right Concentration – the balanced equanimous mind, emotional serenity. Serenity is where the emotions are balanced, supporting each other. They're not going up and down. There's a sense of bliss, of serenity; there is perfect harmony between the intellect, the instincts and the emotions. They're mutually supportive, helping each other. They're no longer conflicting or taking us to extremes and, because of that, we begin to feel a tremendous peacefulness in our minds. There is a sense of ease and fearlessness coming from the Eightfold Path – a sense of equanimity and emotional balance. We feel at ease rather than that sense of anxiety, that tension and emotional conflict. There is clarity; there is peacefulness, stillness, knowing. This insight of the Eightfold Path should be developed; this is *bhavana*. We use the word *bhavana* to signify development.

ASPECTS OF MEDITATION

This reflectiveness of mind or emotional balance is developed as a result of practising concentration and mindfulness meditation. For instance, you can experiment during a retreat and spend one hour doing *samatha* meditation where you are just concentrating your mind on one object, say the sensation of breathing. Keep bringing it into consciousness and sustain it so that it actually has a continuity of presence in the mind.

In this way, you are moving towards what is going on in your own body rather than being pulled out into objects of the senses. If you do not have any refuge within, then you are constantly going out, being absorbed into books, food and all sorts of distractions. But this endless movement of the mind is very exhausting. So instead, the practice becomes one of observing the breath – which means that you have to withdraw or not follow the tendency to find something outside of your-self. You have to bring your attention to the breathing of your own body and concentrate the mind on that sensation. As you let go of gross form, you actually become that feeling, that very sign itself. Whatever you absorb into, you become that for a period of time. When you really concentrate, you have become that very tranquillised condition. You have become tranquil. This is what we call becoming. Samatha meditation is a becoming process.

But that tranquillity, if you investigate it, is not satisfactory tranquillity. There is something missing in it because it is dependent on a technique, on being attached and holding on, on something that still begins and ends. What you become, you can only become temporarily because becoming is a changing thing. It is not a permanent condition. So whatever you become, you will unbecome. It is not ultimate reality. No matter how high you might go in concentration, it will always be an unsatisfactory condition. Samatha meditation takes you to some very high and radiant experiences in your mind – but they all end.

Then, if you practise *vipassana* meditation for another hour by just being mindful and letting go of everything and accepting the uncertainty, the silence and the cessation of conditions, the result is that you will feel peaceful rather than tranquil. And that peacefulness is a perfect peacefulness. It is complete. It is not the tranquillity from *samatha*, which has something imperfect or unsatisfactory about it even at it's best. The realisation of cessation, as you develop that and understand that more and more, brings you true peacefulness, non-attachment, Nibbana.

Thus *samatha* and *vipassana* are the two divisions in medi-tation. One is developing concentrated states of mind on refined objects in which your consciousness becomes refined through that concentration. But being terribly refined, having a great intellect and a taste for great beauty, makes anything coarse unbearable because of the attachment to what is refined. People who have devoted their lives to refinement only find life terribly frustrating and frightening when they can no longer maintain such high standards.

RATIONALITY AND EMOTION

If you love rational thought and are attached to ideas and perceptions, then you tend to despise the emotions. You can notice this tendency if, when you start to feel emotions, you say, 'I'm going to shut it out. I don't want to feel those things.' You don't like to be feeling anything because you can get into a kind of high from the purity of intelligence and the pleasure of rational thinking. The mind relishes the way it is logical and controllable, the way it makes sense. It is just so clean and neat and precise like mathematics – but the emotions are all over the place, aren't they? They are not precise, they are not neat and they can easily get out of control.

So the emotional nature is often despised. We are fright-·· ened of it. For example, men often feel very frightened of emotions because we are brought up to believe that men do not cry. As a little boy, at least in my generation, we were taught that boys do not cry so we'd try to live up to the standards of what boys are supposed to be. They would say, 'You are a boy', and so we'd try to be what our parents said we should be. The ideas of the society affect our minds, and because of that, we find emotions embarrassing. Here in England, people generally find emotions very embarrassing; if you get a little too emotional, they assume that you must be Italian or some other nationality.

If you are very rational and you have figured everything out, then you don't know what to do when people get emotional. If somebody starts crying, you think, 'What am I supposed to do?' Maybe you say, 'Cheer up; it's all right, dear. It'll be all right, there's nothing to cry about.' If you are very attached to rational thought, then you just tend to dismiss it with logic, but emotions do not respond to logic. Often they *react* to logic, but they do not *respond*. Emotion is a very sensitive thing and it works in a way that we sometimes do not comprehend. If we have never really studied or tried to understand what it is to feel life, and really opened and allowed ourselves to be sensitive, then emotional things are very frightening and embarrassing to us. We don't know what they are all about because we have rejected that side of ourselves.

On my thirtieth birthday, I realised that I was an emotionally undeveloped man. It was an important birthday for me. I realised that I was a full grown, mature man – I no longer considered myself a youth, but emotionally, I think I was about six years old some of the time. I really had not developed on that level very much. Even though I could maintain the kind of poise and presence of a mature man in society, I did not always feel that way. I still had very strong unresolved feelings and fears in my mind. It became apparent that I had to do something about that, as the thought that I might have to spend the rest of my life at the emotional age of six was quite a dreary prospect.

This is where many of us in our society get stuck. For example, American society does not allow you to develop emotionally, to mature. It does not understand that need at all, so it does not provide any rites of passage for men. The society does not provide that kind of introduction into a mature world; you are expected to be immature your whole life. You are supposed to *act* mature, but you are not expected to *be* mature. Therefore, very few people are. Emotions are not really understood or resolved – their childish tendencies are merely suppressed rather than developed into maturity.

What meditation does is to offer a chance to mature on the emotional plane. Perfect emotional maturity would be *samma vayama, samma sati* and *samma samadhi*. This is a reflection; you will not find this in any book – it is is for you to contemplate. Perfect emotional maturity comprises Right Effort, Right Mindfulness and Right Concentration. It is present when one is not caught in fluctuations and vicissitudes, where one has balance and clarity and is able to be receptive and sensitive.

THINGS AS THEY ARE

With Right Effort, there can be a cool kind of acceptance of a situation rather than the panic that comes from thinking that it's up to me to set everybody straight, make everything right and solve everybody's problems. We do the best we can, but we also realise that it's not up to us to do everything and make everything right.

At one time when I was at Wat Pah Pong with Ajahn Chah, I could see a lot of things going wrong in the monastery. So I went up to him and I said, 'Ajahn Chah, these things are going wrong; you've got to do something about it.' He looked at me and he said, 'Oh, you suffer a lot, Sumedho. You suffer a lot. It'll change.' I thought, 'He doesn't care! This is the monastery that he's devoted his life to and he's just letting it go down the drain!' But he was right. After a while it began to change and, through just bearing with it, people began to see what they were doing. Sometimes we have to let things go down the drain in order for people to see and to experience that. Then we can learn how not to go down the drain.

Do you see what I mean? Sometimes situations in our life are just *this* way. There's nothing one can do so we allow them to be that way; even if they get worse, we allow them to get worse. But it's not a fatalistic or negative thing we're doing; it's a kind of patience – being willing to bear with something; allowing it to change naturally rather than egotistically trying to prop everything up and cleaning it all up out of our aversion and distaste for a mess.

Then, when people push our buttons, we're not always offended, hurt or upset by the things that happen, or shattered and destroyed by the things that people say or do. One person I know tends to exaggerate everything. If something goes wrong today, she will say, 'I'm utterly and absolutely shattered!'

66

– when all that has happened is that some little problem occurred. However, her mind exaggerates it to such an extent that a very small thing can absolutely destroy her for the day. When we see this, we should realise that there is a great imbalance because little things should not totally shatter anyone.

I realised that I could be easily offended so I took a vow not to be offended. I had noticed how easy it was for me to be offended by little things, whether intentional or unintentional. We can see how easy it is to feel hurt, wounded, offended, upset or worried – how something in us is always trying to be nice, but always feels a little offended by this or a little hurt by that.

With reflection, you can see that the world is like this; it's a sensitive place. It is not always going to soothe you and make you feel happy, secure and positive. Life is full of things that can offend, hurt, wound or shatter. This is life. It is this way. If somebody speaks in a cross tone of voice, you are going to feel it. But then the mind can go on and be offended: 'Oh, it really hurt when she said that to me; you know, that was not a very nice tone of voice. I felt quite wounded. I've never done anything to hurt her.' The proliferating mind goes on like that, doesn't it – you have been shattered, wounded or offended! But then if you contemplate, you realise it's just sensitivity.

When you contemplate this way, it is not that you are trying not to feel. When somebody talks to you in an unkind tone of voice, it's not that you don't feel it at all. We are not trying to be insensitive. Rather, we are trying not to give it the wrong interpretation, not to take it on a personal level. Having balanced emotions means that people can say things that are offensive and you can take it. You have the balance and emotional strength not to be offended, wounded or shattered by what happens in life.

If you are someone who is always being wounded or offended by life, you always have to run off and hide or you have to find a group of obsequious sycophants to live with, people who say: 'You're wonderful, Ajahn Sumedho.' 'Am I really wonderful?' 'Yes, you are.' 'You're just saying that, aren't you?' 'No, no, I mean it from the bottom of my heart.' 'Well, that person over there doesn't think I'm wonderful.' 'Well, he's stupid!' 'That's what I thought.' It's like the story of the emperor's new clothes, isn't it? You have to seek special environments so that everything is affirmed for you – safe and not threatening in any way.

HARMONY

When there is Right Effort, Right Mindfulness and Right Concentration, then one is fearless. There is fearlessness because there is nothing to be frightened of. One has the guts to look at things and not take them in the wrong way; one has the wisdom to contemplate and reflect upon life; one has the security and confidence of *sila*, the strength of one's moral commitment and the determination to do good and refrain from doing evil with body and speech. In this way, the whole thing holds together as a path for development. It is a perfect path because everything is helping and supporting; the body, the emotional nature (the sensitivity of feeling), and the intelligence. They are all in perfect harmony, supporting each other.

Without that harmony, our instinctual nature can go all over the place. If we have no moral commitment, then our instincts can take control. For example, if we just follow sexual desire without any reference to morality, then we become caught up in all kinds of things that cause self-aversion. There is adultery, promiscuity and disease, and all the disruption and confusion that come from not reining in our instinctual nature through the limitations of morality.

We can use our intelligence to cheat and lie, can't we, but when we have a moral foundation, we are guided by wisdom and by *samadhi*; these lead to emotional balance and emotional strength. But we don't use wisdom to suppress sensitivity. We don't dominate our emotions by thinking and by suppressing

68

our emotional nature. This is what we have tended to do in the West; we've used our rational thoughts and ideals to dominate and suppress our emotions, and thus become insensitive to things, to life and to ourselves.

However, in the practice of mindfulness through *vipassana* meditation, the mind is totally receptive and open so that it has this fullness and an all-embracing quality. And because it is open, the mind is also reflective. When you concentrate on a point, your mind is no longer reflective – it is absorbed into the quality of that object. The reflective ability of the mind comes through mindfulness, whole-mindedness. You are not filtering out or selecting. You are just noting whatever arises ceases. You contemplate that if you are attached to anything that arises, it ceases. You have the experience that even though it might be attractive while it is arising, it changes towards cessation. Then it's attractiveness diminishes and we have to find something else to absorb into.

The thing about being human is that we have to touch the earth, we have to accept the limitations of this human form and planetary life. And just by doing that, then the way out of suffering isn't through getting out of our human experience by living in refined conscious states, but by embracing the totality of all the human and *Brahma* realms through mindfulness. In this way, the Buddha pointed to a total realisation rather than a temporary escape through refinement and beauty. This is what the Buddha means when he is pointing the way to Nibbana.

THE EIGHTFOLD PATH AS A REFLECTIVE TEACHING

In this Eightfold Path, the eight elements work like eight legs supporting you. It is not like: 1, 2, 3, 4, 5, 6, 7, 8 on a linear scale; it is more of a working together. It is not that you develop *pañña* first and then when you have *pañña*, you can develop your *sila*; and once your *sila* is developed, then you will have *samadhi*. That is how we think, isn't it: 'You have to have one, then two and then three.' As an actual realisation, developing the Eightfold Path is an experience in a moment, it is all one. All the parts are working as one strong development; it is not a linear process – we might think that way because we can only have one thought at a time.

Everything I have said about the Eightfold Path and the Four Noble Truths is only a reflection. What is really important is for you to realise what I am actually doing as I reflect rather than to grasp the things that I am saying. It is a process of bringing the Eightfold Path into your mind, using it as a reflective teaching so that you can consider what it really means. Don't just think you know it because you can say, 'Samma ditthi means Right Understanding. Samma sankappa means Right Thought.' This is intellectual understanding. Someone might say, 'No, I think samma sankappa means. . . .' And you answer, 'No, in the book it says Right Thought. You've got it wrong.' That is not reflection.

We can translate samma sankappa as Right Thought or Attitude or Intention; we try things out. We can use these tools for contemplation rather than thinking that they are absolutely fixed, and that we have to accept them in an orthodox style; any kind of variation from the exact interpretation is heresy. Sometimes our minds do think in that rigid way, but we are trying to transcend that way of thinking by developing a mind that moves around, watches, investigates, considers, wonders and reflects.

I am trying to encourage each one of you to be brave enough to wisely consider the way things are rather than have someone tell you whether you are ready or not for enlightenment. But actually, the Buddhist teaching is one of being enlightened now rather than doing anything to become enlightened. The idea that you must do something to become enlightened can only come from wrong understanding. Then enlightenment is merely another condition dependent upon something else – so it is not really enlightenment. It is only a perception of enlightenment. However, I am not talking about any kind of perception but about being alert to the way things are. The present moment is what we can actually observe: we can't observe tomorrow yet, and we can only *remember* yesterday. But Buddhist practice is very immediate to the here and now, looking at the way things are.

Now how do we do that? Well, first we have to look at our doubts and fears – because we get so attached to our views and opinions that these take us into doubt about what we are doing. Someone might develop a false confidence believing that they are enlightened. But believing that you are enlightened or believing that you are not enlightened are both delusions. What I am pointing to is *being* enlightened rather than believing in it. And for this, we need to open to the way things are.

We start with the way things are as they happen to be right now – such as the breathing of our own bodies. What has that to do with Truth, with enlightenment? Does watching my breath mean that I am enlightened? But the more you try to think about it and figure out what it is, the more uncertain and insecure you'll feel. All we can do in this conventional form is to let go of delusion. That is the practice of the Four Noble Truths and the development of the Eightfold Path.

Glossary

Ajahn   the Thai word for 'teacher'; often used as the title of the senior monk or monks at a monastery. This is also spelt 'achaan', 'acharn' (and several other ways – all derived from the Pali word 'acariya').

bhikkhu   alms mendicant; the term for a monk, who lives on alms and abides by training precepts which define a life of renunciation and morality.

Buddha rupa   an image of the Buddha

dependent origination   a step-by-step presentation of how suffering arises dependent on ignorance and desire, and ceases with their cessation.

dhamma   a phenomenon when seen as an aspect of the universe, rather than identified with as personal. When capitalised, it refers to the teaching of the Buddha as contained in the scriptures or the Ultimate Truth towards which the teaching points. (In Sanskrit: 'dharma')

kamma   action or cause which is created or recreated by habitual impulse, volitions, natural energies. In popular usage, it often includes the sense of the result or effect of the action, although the proper term for this is *vipaka*. (In Sanskrit: karma)

Observance Day   (in Pali: *Uposatha*) a sacred day or 'sabbath', occurring every lunar fortnight. On this day, Buddhists re-affirm their Dhamma practice in terms of precepts and meditation.

Tipitaka   literally 'three baskets' – the collections of the Buddhist scriptures, classified according to Sutta (Discourses), Vinaya (Discipline or Training) and Abhidhamma (Metaphysics).

The Four Noble Truths

Printed by 倡印者:

The Buddhist Association of the United States

美國佛教會

3070 Albany Crescent,
Bronx, NY 10463
Tel: (718)884-9111

非賣品

歡迎助印

July , 2001.   6000 Copies

The printing is made possible by the following donation
(助印徵信: 美金):

$1200:   慈輝(佛教)基金會
$250:   Zen Palate (禪味)
$200:   BAUS (美國佛教會)
$150:   黃盧秋香

For Free Distribution